Today I Left the House

Today I Left the House

Diary of a First-Time Mom

SARAH M. WHITE

RESOURCE *Publications* · Eugene, Oregon

TODAY I LEFT THE HOUSE
Diary of a First-Time Mom

Resource Publications
An Imprint of Wipf and Stock Publishers
199 W. 8th Ave., Suite 3
Eugene, OR 97401

www.wipfandstock.com

PAPERBACK ISBN: 979-8-3852-0009-2
HARDCOVER ISBN: 979-8-3852-0010-8
EBOOK ISBN: 979-8-3852-0011-5

01/05/24

For new moms
everywhere

And for CG—
I love you more
than a thousand boxes
of chocolate donuts.

You are much loved.

There's no one quite like you.

Now go and fly as only you can.

—GINA OCHSNER

I had never liked babies.

In my visions of motherhood
the child was always eight
and we played with perler beads
at the kitchen table while
listening to "American Pie."

My friends had natural births.
One delivered both her kids naturally
and told me, "You'll be fine."
Another rowed crew in college
and her husband described how
the veins in her neck popped out
like the Incredible Hulk
when she pushed out their son.
We sipped Thai coffee
on her porch—the birth
had gone smoothly,
the baby was eating well.

I saw someone breastfeed a baby
in the church nursery once;
I watched my mother pump
when my brother was born.
Both seemed fairly straightforward.

Still, I wished I could skip
the baby phase and have
an eight-year-old instead. Did a
primal instinct sleep inside
so that when the baby cried
we would know what she needed?
Or would we stand there
staring and bewildered
as she emptied the room's oxygen?

I MET MY HUSBAND CALEB
in the East Towne Mall parking lot
on our way to college orientation.
We were newly eighteen.
I said I would remember
his name because he was tall.
This put him on edge, and he
tried hard to remember mine.
In our first picture together
we sat on logs by a campfire
while he told me about
growing up in São Paulo, Brazil.
Years later, I fell in love with him
because of his goodness.
We married right after college
and he took a job in Madison,
the city where we first met.
Over the next seven years,
we worked and traveled.
We always wanted kids.
I was thinking maybe five
but we weren't in any hurry.

I FIRST WANTED A BABY
after we spent time
with our friends'
eight-month-old.
He chose me
the way babies do.
He flirted and cooed.
We sat together
at his kitchen table.
I cut cubes of pear
that he grabbed
with pudgy fingers
and I thought,
"How hard can this be?"

IN MY FIRST ADULT LIFE
I taught high school Spanish
which meant I spent all day
coaxing teenagers to forget
they had never wanted
to learn a second language.

After I announced I was pregnant,
one of my ninth-grade girls
kept reminding me, "Mrs. White,
you know how that baby's
going to come out, right?"

"I can't turn back now," I said.

I hung a colorful poster
on my whiteboard
for students to guess
boy or girl for candy.
Most scrawled their initials
in the boy column. "Do they all
prefer boys?" I wondered.
"Do they think *I* do?"
When the baby was a girl,
they were disappointed,
but I saved on candy.

When coworkers asked
how I was feeling,
I complained about
not sleeping.

They didn't sympathize.

Since Caleb and I like
to be prepared, we attended
every class on offer at the hospital—
the birth class, breastfeeding,
and care of the newborn.

In the birth class we learned
each phase of labor had a clear
number of hours and centimeters.
Later on, I used this information
to create a labor-tracking chart
to time my passage through
the various phases and centimeters.

We learned the PAIN acronym:
purposeful,
anticipated,
intermittent,
normal.

The birth video followed two women.
One woman engaged in the process
and moved around in different positions.
The other lay expressionless on the bed
and then asked for an epidural.
It was clear which method
the hospital favored.

I first learned about epidurals
from my sociology professor
who said you couldn't feel
when to push and the baby
couldn't feel anything either.
I still don't know if this is true.

The woman on-screen who chose
a natural birth appeared almost
buoyant as she began her labor.
She swayed in her living room
and bent over the back of the couch.
At the hospital, she breathed
through her tough contractions, but then,
in transition, she hung her head
as hair fell from her ponytail
around her flushed face and she whimpered,
"I can't do it. I can't take anymore."

For me, the question of a natural birth
was decided at age five when I kicked,
screamed, crawled under the chair,
and had to be dragged out
and held down by the nurses
for my kindergarten shots.

I thought this woman was
incredibly brave to be
filmed while giving birth,
but when she almost gave up
so near the end, I understood:
natural birth would break me.
I watched in awe as she rallied.

"Let's practice breathing," said the nurse.
Everyone spread out and the women
assumed various labor positions.
"Now, visualize a happy place," she said.
I imagined a spot at the end
of a fjord in Flåm, Norway,
before I decided there was no way
I could take this exercise seriously.
"Maybe I'll try this when I'm
actually in labor," I thought,
doubting it would counteract real pain.
But as I scanned the room,
everyone else was going with it.

AT MY BABY SHOWER
I asked for encouraging notes.

Two favorites from friends
without children read:

You always know what to do.
I've always looked up to you
as someone who was
incredibly competent at life.
I know it will be the same
with motherhood.

and

When you don't feel prepared or able,
remember your God is near and able.

I felt as prepared as I could be.
I knew problems might come up,
but I believed everything would work
the way it was supposed to.

I didn't know my preparation
would be useless, I would see God
in the kindness of healthcare workers,
and all my competence was about to fade.

I DECIDED TO TAKE A BREAK
from teaching while I adjusted
to motherhood, as in,
I quit my job.

My baby girl wasn't due
until June 25th.
The first week of summer,
I went into school every day
to clean out my classroom.
I sorted and labeled
each scrap of lesson
into two giant binders
for the next teacher.
I cleaned out the cabinets.
I turned in my key and left.

Finally, time to relax.
I could get a pedicure.
I could go to my favorite
coffee shop and write.
I could sit on the couch
and eat ice cream every night
for the next two weeks.

Or so I thought.

"Hey, Caleb, wake up."
I shook his shoulder.
"My water just broke."

"What?" he said. "What time is it?"

"It's three in the morning," I said.

"Are you sure?" he asked.
"It's two weeks early."

"Yeah," I said. "I'm sure.
It was the gush of fluids
they ask about
at every appointment."

"You call the hospital," he said.
"I'll finish packing the stuff."

"They said we should come in," I said.

"This is exciting!" he said with a big smile.

"We should have gone to bed before midnight."

WHILE CALEB DROVE
the empty highway
I used an app
to track my contractions,
but I couldn't tell
if I was having one.
Occasionally, I felt
a dull ache, like a cramp.

"What's happening over there?" Caleb asked.

"Not much," I said.
"I think they're stopping,
but it's hard to tell."

Caleb parked in the hospital garage.
He grabbed our bags, and we started
the mile-long walk to the birth suites.
If I ever design a hospital, the birth suites
will be just inside the main entrance.
We made this trek for every class
as my belly grew. When we
crossed over the sky bridge
I realized it was the last time
we would cross as only two.
The next time, we would be three.

WE CHECKED INTO THE BIRTH SUITES
and were admitted to a triage room.

The nurse at triage said,
"Since you haven't started regular contractions,
we'll just make sure your water broke."

"What else could it be?" I asked.

"Pee," she smiled and shrugged
as if people peed on themselves
all the time without realizing it.

AFTER THEY DECIDED
I hadn't peed on myself,
they wanted to get the baby out
within twenty-four hours,
so they set me up for induction
with the labor-inducing drug Pitocin.

It's better if I don't look
when the nurse prepares the needle,
so I studied the second hand
above the door. I felt the poke,
then something warm and wet
on my pants and my foot.
Caleb rushed over and wiped
me off with paper towels.

Before the birth, Caleb received only
one piece of advice from a coworker:
"Don't wear shoes to the birth
that you want to keep."
When Caleb shared this with me,
I said, "That's ridiculous!"
Now at least one favorite sandal
was soaked with blood.

Caleb cleaned me off
while the nurse taped down
my IV. She apologized
over and over. She was
so flustered she forgot
to label the vials of blood.

Ten minutes later, a lab tech
wheeled her cart into the room
and asked for more blood.

"Where is my other blood?" I demanded.
"What happened to my other blood?"

"It wasn't labeled with your e-number.
We can't use it. It's protocol," she said.

I sent Caleb a strong back-me-up stare,
but he works in healthcare software,
and it was protocol.

WHILE WE WAITED IN EARLY LABOR
for contractions to pick up,
we watched twelve bakers
push bread in and out of ovens.
I was so bored I asked the nurse,
"So, what do people
usually do during this part?"
She suggested walking the floor.
We grinned at each other
as we pushed my Pitocin drip.
Whenever we passed
the central nurses' station,
one of them looked up
and smiled back at us.
Our smiles said excitement.
Their smiles said something else,
something like, "They have no idea.
Bless their little hearts."

I BROUGHT CHARTS AND MARKERS
to track the stages of labor.
I wanted to visualize my progress,
like checking off a to-do list.
Fifteen hours had already passed
and all I had to show for it was
a measly five centimeters.
I thought the whole birth would
be over in fifteen hours!
I was in no mood for shading.
Neither the nurse or the resident
expressed surprise or concern
at how long it was taking.
Even Caleb was going with the flow.
I missed my own OB who wasn't
on call. She was leaving the hospital
when I arrived and stopped by
to check on me at the beginning.
"Try not to watch the clock," she said.

I CHOSE NITROUS OXIDE
from the hospital's
pain relief menu,
but the tubes were
out of stock.

I felt cold
so my nurse wrapped me
in a warm sheet.

I felt nauseous
so she gave me
a blue plastic ring
with a barf bag.

My legs shook involuntarily.
There was nothing
she could do about that.

"I NEED A BREAK,"
I said at ten p.m.
the next evening,
nineteen hours in,
too tired to focus.

I climbed into the bed,
dug my knees into
the floppy mattress,
and rested my forehead
on the headboard.

Dilaudid, an analgesic narcotic,
trickled through my IV.
It was supposed to help me relax
and take the edge off the pain.

"How's that?" asked my nurse.

Another contraction ripped
through my back and abdomen.
"I still feel it," I said.
"Give me the full dose."

I drifted in the dark
until pain brought me back.
"Pressure," I called out.
Hands braced my back.

I sank into pure,
soft blackness.

I WAITED FOR THE WAVE,
held my breath,
tipped my chin
to my chest
and pushed.

Any sound I made
was a humming growl
from the back of my throat
so no air escaped.

I could never remember
whether to push or pull
on the white handles
that popped magically
out of the bed
like a torture chair.

With every push
her head came
down,
down,
down,
then up.

She would not stay.
For five hours.

The perplexed resident
watched for a while, and said,
"Why don't you try
going to the bathroom
one more time."

Then she left.

THE RESIDENT SAT CALMLY
on a stool at my feet
and held back my skin
around the baby's head.
The entire hospital staff gathered
for this one moment of searing,
burning pain—the ring of fire.
"Isn't there anything
you can do?" I pleaded.
Surely they had a spray for this.
They shook their heads.

Finally
the doctor started
to count me through:
"Deep breath in.
Now, push. One, two,
three, four, five . . .
Good. Breathe.
Now, push."
We did it all again.
And again.
Caleb cheered
for every push
as if it were the last one.
"Breathe. Now, push.
One, two, three, good,
four, five, don't stop,

six, seven, keep pushing!
There's the head.
Keep pushing.
Push again. Push. *Push.*
There's the shoulders.
There she is!"

The doctor held her up
and said to Caleb,
"It's a . . ."
Caleb already knew
we were having a girl,
so it took him a minute
to respond, ". . . girl?"
"Yes," said the doctor,
offering Caleb the cord to cut.

They set her warm, wet body
on my chest, and she wailed
while they wiped her off.
I put my hand on her back
and said, "It's okay, it's okay, it's okay."

I studied her while she cried.
She was smaller than I had imagined.
A purple line marked her forehead
from where she had hit something
on her way out. One of my bones?

Caleb stood beside us in tears
and said, "You were amazing."

She calmed and opened her eyes.
"It's a miracle," I said.
People always used that word,
but I hadn't understood until
I clutched her to my chest
and felt her living weight.

And then she pooped on me
as if to say, "Hello, world.
This is my mom. I stamp her
with my poop." I didn't mind.

THE NURSE AT OUR BIRTH CLASS HAD SAID,
"You won't notice the stitches
because you'll be holding your baby."

That is a lie.

You will also notice the staff
joking among themselves
about how many doctors it takes
to open a bottle of lidocaine.

THE NURSES PUT EYE SALVE ON HER EYES,
wrapped her tightly, and gave her to Caleb
while I scarfed buttered toast.
Somehow, I got into a wheelchair.
The nurse put the baby on a pillow
on my lap, wheeled us to a room,

and left us

alone

with the baby.

WE WERE IN SHOCK
and hadn't slept
for a long time.

"What will we
call her?" I asked Caleb.

"After that,
you can name her
anything you want."

My mother arrived.

Caleb had called her
at the beginning of labor.
"Oh! She's early!" she said
and began her drive
from Memphis.

Twenty-seven hours
was enough time for her
to pack her bags,
drive for two days,
sleep in a hotel,
and arrive refreshed
to hold her first
granddaughter
hours after
she was born.

We planned for her
to stay a few weeks
and help with meals,
baby care, and naps.
We both felt clueless,
but she knew what to do.

CALEB SLEPT BESIDE ME.
My mom slept at our house.
The nurse wouldn't return
for another two hours.

But I couldn't sleep.

When I closed my eyes
I saw the birth as if from above:
the part when I vomited
into the blue plastic bag,
the part when I crumpled
into a ball after the nurse's fingers
numbered my cervix at seven centimeters,
the blaring lights like shattered glass,
the ceiling mirror where they claimed
I could see her crowning
if I looked closely enough.

I opened my eyes.

There she was in her plastic box.

FEEDING MY BABY
from a tiny tube
taped to my pinky
wasn't covered
in breastfeeding class.

Before she arrived,
I only worried
she would be ugly,
which seems foolish now.

EVERY NURSE TRIED
to help her latch.
And every nurse
tried to reassure me
after it didn't work:

"She's sleepy
from her high
bilirubin levels."

"She's two weeks early.
Keep trying."

"Colostrum
(the first milk)
takes a lot of work
for newborns
to get out."

"She'll get it for sure
in two or three weeks.
Don't give up."

WE LEFT THE HOSPITAL
with a feeding plan.
We would buy donor milk
until my milk came in.

We established a rhythm at home
with our base in the living room
and all the curtains drawn.

Caleb and my mom took turns
getting up with me at night.
I tried to latch the baby,
then I switched to pumping
while one of them gave her a bottle.

My mom made me banana bread toast
and told me jokes at two a.m.
She changed the baby's diaper,
swaddled her, and put her to bed.

While I bonded with my baby,
I also bonded with my mom.

THE FIRST TIME PUMPING
I felt like Cary Elwes
in *The Princess Bride*:
"I've just sucked
one year of your life away."

The brick-like white box
had two dials and hoses.
No one explained
how to use it. They told me:
"Start it fast, then go slow."
How could a woman
who had never breastfed
comprehend letdown?
This machine was my doom,
but I didn't know that then,
so I bobbed happily
in the living room,
suction cups stuck
to my breasts and parodied
"Pump up the Jam."

You're so cute.
You'reso cute.
You'resocute.

We say it so much
she's going to think
it's her first name.

WE TOOK BABY TO THE DOCTOR
almost every day
because her bilirubin levels
still hadn't come down.

She needed a biliblanket,
and the home health techs
delivered it to our home
and taught us how to use it.

This blanket wasn't soft or cozy,
but a thin, transparent vinyl spatula
filled with rows of ultraviolet lights
for constant phototherapy.

A soft white fabric sleeve
slipped over the spatula base,
and fabric wings wrapped around
baby's chest to hold it in place.

Diaper, biliblanket, onesie,
swaddle—hopefully one
with a hole near the bottom
to let the thick metal cord through.

Baby glowed blue, day and night,
while lights cleared her blood.
I knew it was helping,
but I hated seeing her like that.

I hated seeing her strapped in,
lit up like a sci-fi baby,
attached by a snake hose
to a power outlet.

ONE NIGHT WHEN SHE WOKE
I picked her up, swaddled and shining,
and offered her a breast.

Maybe she will latch this time.

The thick metal power cord
pulled her down, away from me.
Like other times before,
she was not interested.

I stared at her peaceful face a while
before putting her back down.

Maybe next time.

WHEN UNWRAPPED FROM HER SWADDLE
her fists shoot up to the sky
like the pages in a pop-up book.
She's Peter Pan and sometimes
Superman, my flighted being
who grasps handfuls of infinity.

TODAY I LEFT THE HOUSE.
I went to the mailbox.

My list of fears was lengthy:
she could choke on spit-up,
I could drop her,
she could die in the night,
one of us could fall while
carrying her down the stairs
and she would be smashed
to pieces on the wood floor.

Like most of my other fears
(tornadoes, car accidents,
snakes, economic shutdown,
drowning), none of this
ever happened.

What actually happened,
I could not have predicted.

AROUND THE FIFTH DAY
milk and fluids
turned my breasts
from flesh to stone.
Nothing would change them back.
Not ice packs, heat packs,
showers, ibuprofen,
green cabbage leaves,
pumping, hand expression.
Apparently breast care
was a full-time job,
but I just wanted to sleep.
I didn't know what to do.

At baby's bilirubin check-up,
I pointed to the flu warning sign.
"I have everything on that sign."
"It's not flu season," said Caleb.
"Well, then, why did they hang the sign?"
"Okay, we'll call your doctor."

The nurses tried and tried,
but she wouldn't latch.
"She's a tough cookie,"
said the lactation consultant.

Part of me was relieved
they couldn't figure her out either.

I left the room during her heel prick,
but cried in the lobby anyway.
Actually, I had cried every day
since she was born.

Was that normal?

When I called the OB nurse,
she was not concerned
about the mystery fever
since I had no other symptoms,
no pain anywhere. I should take
Tylenol and ibuprofen and see
a doctor if my temperature
rose to one hundred and one.

"COME ON. PLEASE LATCH.
You can do this," I said.

I stroked her top lip
with my nipple
and waited for her
to open wide.
Then I shoved her mouth
over the nipple.
She closed her mouth
and slid off.

I tried again
and again.

"Come on," I pleaded with her.

Nothing happened.

"Sarah, it's been long enough," Caleb said.

"How long has it been?" I asked.

"Fifteen minutes," he said.

"Oh. Okay." I passed him the baby
and strapped on the flanges to pump.

ON A DRIZZLY DAY WE TOOK BABY
on her first neighborhood walk.
It was the day before my birthday.
I felt well enough to go around the block.
"Let's take a picture to post
on Facebook," Caleb said.
We still hadn't announced.
We huddled around
her sleeping frame
tucked in the stroller.
Caleb reached far away
and took a selfie—
we've got our raincoats on
and big grins too. In the photo
I don't look sick, just tired.

ON THE EVENING OF MY BIRTHDAY
our best friends brought over
a Costco birthday cake.
Pregnant, that cake was the best,
but now it tasted like chalk.

After dinner, I felt so cold
I drank a cup of hot water.
Our friends insisted on washing up.
I wished they would leave.

As soon as they left,
I collapsed on the couch
and Caleb took my temperature:
over one hundred and one.

"No, no. I can't go back in," I said.

"Let's just call and see what they say," Caleb said.

"Can you call for me?" I asked.

The OB doctor in the ER wanted to see me.

We took my temperature again:
one hundred and four.

I stopped fighting.

"What about the baby?" I asked.
My mom was in Chicago
at my brother's college graduation.
We called our friends to come back;
they lived a mile away.

I don't remember
Caleb moving the car seat,
loading them with diapers
and clothes, the essentials.

I do remember my friend asking
for my pajama shirt
so the baby could smell me
and be encouraged to eat.

I wanted to say
she's still not nursing
so I doubt my smell
will make any difference.

I held my ten-day's baby,
unsure of when I would
see her again, then someone
took her from me. We drove
the same route as before,
but this time felt
much less hopeful.

IN THE ER WAITING ROOM
the vending machine cover
glowed blue with tantalizing
beads of water. The intake worker
wouldn't let me have any water
because it could affect
my temperature.

I gazed at the fake condensation
while nurses tried to jigsaw
a large woman in a wheelchair
into the bathroom stall.

The triage nurse called my name.

"Wow," said the nurse
as she read the thermometer.
"One hundred and five."

"I've never had a fever
that high," I said.

THE NURSE LED US TO A ROOM
with a sliding glass door
and a curtain and TV.

I changed into a gown,
then two male nurses
took blood and placed an IV
as quickly as they could.
While they worked,
I interviewed them:
"So, how did you become a nurse?"

Three doctors examined me.
One of these doctors told Caleb
he had never seen such a high fever
in an adult, only in children.

The OB doctors asked me
about my breasts:
"Do you have any pain?"
They checked for red patches
and ruled out mastitis.
They ordered a pelvic exam
in case of stowaway placenta,
an ultrasound, and a CT scan.

The CT scan was the only test
that took place in a separate room,
but I don't remember how I got there—
if I walked or if they wheeled me.
I remember a black-and-white wheel
suspended in the air.

I felt so cold. I asked for socks,
but they wouldn't give me a blanket.
Caleb put the socks on my feet
and sat right beside my bed.

While we waited, I recited
all of the prayers I had forced
my students to memorize,
including Psalm 23:
"Even though I walk
through the valley
of the shadow of death,
I will fear no evil,
for you are with me."

They had no idea
what was wrong with me.

AROUND ELEVEN P.M., THE ER DOCTOR
poked his head through the curtain
and said, "Sarah, today's your birthday?"

"I know. It sucks, right?"

LATER, THE ER DOCTOR RETURNED:
"If you hadn't just had a baby,
if you just showed up in the ER
with a fever that high and no symptoms,
I'd be thinking meningitis."

"How do you test for that?" asked Caleb.

"We'd do a lumbar puncture.
It's a pretty similar procedure
to an epidural. You might have had one—"

"No," I interrupted.
"I didn't have one.
I hate needles."

"Oh," said the doctor, dismayed.

"Can you give us a few minutes?" Caleb asked.

"I can't believe this," I said.
"I did the whole birth
only to have to do this now."

"I know," said Caleb.

"But we need to keep ruling things out."

"I feel the same way," said Caleb.

"Okay, I'll do it," I said.

When the ER doctor returned,
I told him, "You can do it,
but I want you to give me
something so I will stay calm
because I hate needles."

"That's fine," he said.
"I'll get you some dilaudid."

I sat with Caleb in front of me
and the doctor and nurses behind.
They gave me some dilaudid,
but I felt no calmer than before.
In this moment I hated who I was
and wished I could be like other people,
like Caleb, a gold-star blood donor.

"Okay, now lean forward," said the doctor.
"Put your elbows on the tray table.
Good. Now stay still—just like that.
It opens up your vertebrae.
You'll feel some pinching—
that's the lidocaine.
Try to relax and breathe."

I imagined one hundred
needles piercing my back.
I tried to stay still
while balancing my elbows
on the cold metal table.

"I'm feeling everything.
I don't think it's numb."

"Okay, I can do more."
He injected more lidocaine.

"We're done," he said.
"See this liquid?"
He held up three vials
of my spinal fluid.
"It's clear.
No meningitis."

I WOKE UP ON THE FOURTH FLOOR.
Caleb slept in a chair beside my bed.
For my first test of the day
I needed a second, larger IV.
My nurse shined a special light
on my forearm and my veins appeared
like a pale tree inside me.
She tried to place the IV,
but every time she was almost there
my vein shut and the needle
wouldn't go any further.
Next, the floor nurse tried and said,
"Your veins are really valve-y."
The PICC nurse finally placed the IV
in my upper arm, ninety minutes later.
I had two IVs and so many bruises.
In the CT scan, the warm contrast dye
whooshed through the new IV
and sent tingling through my limbs
like milk letdown or peeing.
The contrast highlighted
my insides working perfectly.
They still had no idea
what was wrong with me.

WHENEVER THE SHIFT CHANGED
the new nurse asked about my baby:
"Oh, I see you just had a baby!"
Maybe they thought
talking about her
would make it easier
for me to bear
that she wasn't here
and I was stuck
in the hospital.
"Did you have a girl or boy?"
Maybe they thought
it would help me
get better if I held
the image of her face
in my mind
the way I wished
I could hold
her newborn body.
"What's her name?"
Maybe they thought
I would enjoy
a good cry
every single
shift change.

I PUMPED ON THE EDGE
of the bed every few hours,
but I couldn't bend my arm
because of the two IVs.
Caleb left to buy me
a fancy pumping bra.
The milk was contaminated
with the contrast dye,
so we had to throw it away.
My head throbbed when I stood up.
The IV antibiotics made me
poop on myself in the bed.
A nurse who was eight months pregnant
wiped the poop from my leg
and sponged me down.
We chatted about baby names.
She liked the name Hazel.
She was my favorite nurse
because we talked about
her life instead of mine.

Since I couldn't sit or stand
without excruciating
pounding in my head,
Jeremy, the MRI tech,
wheeled me and my bed
to the MRI theater,
which felt like an alternate
hospital universe as
upbeat music filled the room.
He and an assistant
lifted me with a sheet
from my bed onto the MRI tray.
I put on an eye mask
and headphones to block out
the "construction zone clanging"
Jeremy had warned me about.
I purposefully did not look
at the size of the very small tube
before the tray slid me inside
with a mechanical whirring.

"What station?" asked Jeremy.

"How about U2," I said.

I knew every song but one.
Somehow, they kept time
with the machine's clanging.
Each melody reminded me
my life had existed
outside the hospital
and perhaps it could again.

Jeremy: "This next set
is about seven minutes.
You're doing great."

Halfway through the MRI,
he took me out of the tube
and injected the contrast into my IV.
The plank slid me back into the machine.

When the MRI ended, he wheeled me
to my room and said like a benediction,
"I hope you get out of here soon."

OUR FRIENDS STOPPED BY
to pick up some pumped milk
and brought the baby.

I didn't want them to see me,
so Caleb shuffled back and forth
from the room to the hallway.

He brought me the baby,
and I cradled her
in the hospital bed.
Her bright yellow onesie
with white polka dots
hung loosely on her body.
"Hi, sweetie. I miss you
so much. I'm going to
come home soon."
I stroked her dark hair
as she nestled against me.
I sobbed to Caleb,
"I just want to go home
and be with her."

Too soon, the visit ended.
Caleb scooped her up
and carried her to our friends.

He returned and knelt beside my bed.
We grasped hands.
He laid his head on the bed
while his shoulders heaved.

"YOU HAVE MASTITIS,"
said a new OB on a new shift,
like it was completely obvious
and we were all idiots
not to have figured it out by now.

Every nonmedical person
had already guessed mastitis:
first-time mom,
non-latching baby,
bad breast pump,
flu-like symptoms.

It was obvious.
It was obvious now.

While she drew a box
around the red patch on my breast
with a black felt-tip marker,
I wanted to say, "That wasn't there before."

"You can go home once you're fever-free,
and I'm sending you a hospital-grade pump."

"My baby still isn't latching," I told the consultant.

She explained how to use the new pump
and gave me the usual pep talk but added,
"Don't try at every feeding.
Try it a few times a day for five minutes
when you're both in a good mood.
Stop when one of you gets frustrated."

Her permission not to try
lifted the pressure.

THE FINAL HURDLE WAS
a breast ultrasound.
No abscess; instead,
a "vague phlegmon,"
or soft tissue inflammation.
They ordered a repeat
scan in two weeks.

But they let me go home.

ALL I WANT TO DO
is hold my baby.

So, I do.

I sit with her
at three a.m.
and marvel.
I stare into
her eyes,
her face.
She is mine
and I am here.
We are here
together
in the middle
of the night
and there is
no place
I have to be
tomorrow
except
with her.

I was home,
but the headache
screamed on.
I could barely
sit at the table.

No hospital doctor
had addressed it—
maybe it was from
the spinal tap,
maybe not.

I made an appointment
with anyone at primary care
who could see me immediately.

Caleb drove me to the clinic
with the passenger seat
tipped all the way back.

The nurse practitioner
prescribed Vicodin for the pain
but also said I could have
a rebound headache
from all the ibuprofen.
I stopped taking it immediately.

We picked up the Vicodin,
but I stashed it in a kitchen drawer
and never took a single dose
because I was afraid
I would get addicted.
I had watched *House*.
I knew what could happen.

THE HEADACHE FADED.

I wanted to forget,
but scattered bruises
up and down my arms
caught me in the mirror.

In the shower, I scrubbed
at the gunky tape residue,
but it clung to me.

There was
no class
for this.

Newborns open social doors;
people speak to you compulsively,
so that by the time you have reached
the back aisle with the bulk Bounty
paper towels, you will have heard:
"Oh! How precious!"
"They grow up so fast!"
"There's nothing like it!"
as if you were not strangers at Costco,
but intimate friends.

Then you never see them again.

My mom's parents
called to check in.

My grandpa joked,
"Is she crawling yet?"
Joy twinkled in his voice.

"Not yet," I said.

"You can name
the next one Samantha
because it has 'Sam'
and 'Ann' in it," he said.

"We'll see," I said.

He passed the phone
back to my grandma
who said she would
keep us updated on
his upcoming surgery
to fix a bleeding problem.

THE FIRST TIME SHE LATCHED
we sat in the basement
on the brown leather couch
watching *Eureka*.

I tried on a whim.

"Look," I said quietly.
"She's doing it."

"Yeah!" said Caleb. "Woohoo!"

From the other couch
my mom confessed,
"I thought she never would,"
like releasing a held breath.

Her admission surprised me.
I had believed the nurses—
she would latch eventually—
because that was all I knew
to believe. And if my mom
had exhaled any sooner
I might have given up.

THE A/C BROKE THE NEXT DAY.
It was eighty-five inside
by the time the technician fixed it,
so we had baby's first basement campout
with Mom and Dad on the air mattress
and baby in the pack and play.

There were no s'mores.

A BREASTFEEDING PRIMER

1.
I am a milk machine.
I make it night and day.
There is no end to me.
I am a milk machine.

2.
Babies are equipped with nipple radar
so that at any moment they can detect
the location of either nipple
and scratch it with their claws.

3.
The water glass is always
just out of   reach.

4.
Breast milk baptizes everything you own:
clothing, furniture, carpet, bedspread, walls.
It's the new flavor of your home
like a scented candle.

5.
Don't kiss me right now.
I've already got one set of lips on me.

DREAM SCENE ONE:
I am feeding my baby.
She has Medusa hair.
I hate snakes.

Dream scene two:
I am feeding my baby.
Her hair is bright green
iridescent leaves
from her crinkle book.

Dream scene three:
I am feeding my baby.
Four miniature fangs poke out
at the corners of her gums.

Before I had the baby
the first-grade teacher found
a pack of unused cloth diapers
in a giveaway box. "These make
the best burp rags," she said,
handing me the package.

I underestimated how important
a good burp rag would be.
I did not expect my baby
to frequently throw up
entire feedings all over me,
the furniture, her clean outfit, etc.
I did not expect to be soaked
to my underwear in spit-up.

At one in the morning, all of the milk
splattered onto the carpet so violently
that it splashed onto the hem of my pants.

"Caleb," I called. "Wake up. I need you
to help me clean spit-up out of the carpet."

He grabbed a roll of paper towels
and we squatted, mopping it up
groggy and mechanical,
the glory of parenting.

I COMPLETED ALL MY FOLLOW-UPS AT ONCE:

The ultrasound tech measured
the "vague phlegmon" again,
but the dark orb was unchanged.
The radiologist could not say what it was—
a swollen lymph node?

I failed the depression screener from my OB
when I answered questions like
"Are you getting enough sleep?"
and "Do you feel hopeful?"

Who writes these questions?

At least I felt more hopeful
than when I was hospitalized.

My OB reviewed the ultrasound and prescribed
more antibiotics and a visit to a surgeon.
"No one gets hospitalized for mastitis.
We usually give antibiotics over the phone.
Your case is very atypical."

My grandma called again,
this time to say my grandpa's surgery
to fix a bleeding problem was successful,
but his lungs wouldn't start again.

Would my mother please
come down to Memphis
to say goodbye?

They were waiting for her.

Caleb was at work.

"What am I going to do?" she asked.
"Should I fly or drive?"

"It's eleven hours," I said. "Let's look at tickets.
Or we could wait until Caleb gets home."

She thought about it, then said,
"I just need to get in the car and drive."

We threw her shoes into a duffel bag
and loaded her car while wiping our faces—
the double blow of his loss and hers.

IT'S A SIX-HUNDRED-
sixty-eight-mile drive
from Madison to Memphis.
Multiply by one nursing infant

and two anxious,
rule-following parents
and it might as well be
two thousand miles.

I remembered road trips
to Florida with my parents
who let us lie down
on the floor between seats.

I imagined mothers of the past
breastfeeding on the leather bench
seat of a sprawling sedan
or maybe even behind the wheel.

Now, it's drive two hours, stop one,
six hundred sixty-eight miles.

ON ROAD TRIP DAY ONE,
I had a plugged duct,
but I couldn't say anything
because we had picked up
my young, single brother
on our way through Rockford.
They sat together in the front
distracted by the approaching storm.
I sat in the back with baby.

Front seat: "Wow! Did you
see that lightning?"

Back seat (furiously massaging
and googling): "Can you please drive faster?"

Front seat: "No. It's really windy right now."

As a novice with two week's
breastfeeding experience,
I searched the internet a lot.
It was mainly unhelpful.
I didn't learn until years later
that breast massage
damages the tissue.

Back seat: "I think we should
stop now so I can feed the baby."

Front seat: "Whoa! Cool lightning!"

All night in the hotel room
I heated with white washcloths
soaked in hot tap water,
fed the baby, and then cooled
with ice in a clean trash bag.
Still no relief.

I never knew breasts could be
so high maintenance. All my life,
breasts were about form only;
now they had a function,
and with it, personality.

On road trip day two,
we stopped every two hours
so I could feed the baby,
but still I had no relief.

I nursed in a wing chair
in my grandma's bedroom,
and the duct cleared instantly.
Was it the angle of the baby's
mouth or her whole body?
Was it something else?
After two feedings, I was fine.

THE NIGHT BEFORE THE SERVICE
I sat in the upstairs hallway
of my girlhood home
while the house slept.
I tried to write out what to say.
A few minutes wasn't enough
to capture our summer walks
to the snowball stand,
my favorite stewed chicken
on my birthday every year,
and French toast breakfasts.
Food was his language—
the way he built us into people.
When I was home from college
(which he paid for, even though
I went to a Christian college
and they are Reformed Jews),
he would take me out
for avocado-chicken soup
at his favorite Mexican place.
He stood at the dinner table
on his fiftieth wedding anniversary
and said in tears before all the guests
that he loved my grandmother
more than on the day he married her.

When Caleb and I were looking for a house,
he told me, "Get something nice,"
which meant it was okay to spend.
He lived on the same earth with my daughter
for a few weeks, but never got to hold her.

BABIES
brighten up
funerals.

TEACH US TO NUMBER OUR DAYS

My family waits—
Caleb, the baby, and I,
my sister and brother,
my mother and aunt,
my grandmother—
we wait with the rabbi, Katie,
in a small side room.

that we may gain a heart of wisdom.

She offers us black ribbon to tear
as a symbol of rending our garments.

Satisfy us in the morning with your unfailing love

We process into the hall and
take our places in the first row.

that we may sing for joy and be glad all our days.

Katie surprises me by reading Psalm 90,
a very familiar psalm to me,
and part of the Scriptures he and I shared.
I wasn't expecting to be comforted.

May the beauty of the Lord our God rest upon us;

My brother reads an essay on cooking
with Grandpa, and then it's my turn.

establish the work of our hands for us—

I mount the platform and scan the grey heads,
all unknown to me, but all part of their world.
I make it to line three before I have to stop.
I clutch the tissues in one hand
and the edge of the podium with the other.
I start again and make it to the end.

yes, establish the work of our hands.

A WHITE CANOPY BLOCKED THE MEMPHIS HEAT.
We stood on a false ground;
the carpet of vibrant artificial grass
likely covered rows of graves.

When I saw the coffin, I felt a weight
in my stomach as I admitted:
He's in there. I won't see him again.

We sat in white plastic chairs
as the rabbi read the prayers
and invited us to sprinkle dirt.

Not knowing the customs,
I asked if I could touch the coffin.
I placed my whole hand
on the glossy cover and said goodbye.

Many people approached my grandma
where she sat in the first row. Though
not one for tenderness, on this day
she cupped faces in her hands
and held them there, whispering.

I NEVER HEARD
my grandma sing
until I heard her
singing to my baby.

Caleb went to Dubai for work
and I spent a week with my baby
in the house I grew up in.

Nothing went wrong.

We took over the bedroom where
I rewrote *Island of the Blue Dolphins*
in third grade, made lists from
my parents' old baby name book,
and copied Bible verses
onto rainbow stationery to display
on my twin white closet doors:
"Enter through the narrow gate."

Now she slept
in a pack and play
at the foot of the bed
in a happy collision.

IN WEEK SEVEN
back in Madison
I try to follow
a schedule.
This will make
us happier.
I wake my baby
at six a.m. to eat.
She would rather
be sleeping.
So would I.
I make a chart
with rewards
for every day
I drag myself
out of bed
and try to feed
my sleeping baby.
Day one:
Sephora Play!
subscription.
Day two:
New baby outfits.
I give up
by day three.

At my appointment with the general surgeon, she recommended another ultrasound and, in the worst case, a core biopsy.

She warned me, "Since you're nursing there's a risk you might develop a milk fistula— when milk comes out of the incision site."

"What?" I said.
"For how long?"

"I'm not sure," she said.
"None of my patients has ever gotten one."

"So I'll be the first," I thought.

AT THE TWO-MONTH BABY CHECK-UP,
I explained, "I was trying to figure out
why she spits up entire feedings,"
and the pediatrician said,
"This is a laundry problem."

I stared at her, not understanding.

Caleb nodded along.

"You just have to throw
your hands up sometimes.
Your baby weighs twelve pounds."

"Is that good?" I thought.

Later, I would learn that
feeding a baby again
after a thirty-minute nap
was too much. I was giving her
enough milk for three babies.
Her egg-sized stomach couldn't hold it.

"Are you enjoying it at least a little bit?" she asked.

I've never slept less.
Everything is harder
than I thought it would be.
I can't control anything
or plan anything
or fix anything.
I used to be capable.
Now what am I?

"Yes," I said.

"The first twelve weeks are grueling," she said.

TIRED IS WHEN
you order
your dad's
birthday present
and ship it
to yourself.

"Who ordered this
Tazo tea sampler?" I asked.

Three minutes later:
"Oh. I did."

Every Sunday night, I envied Caleb.
In the morning, he could leave.

Where he was going, break rooms
offered adults a short reprieve
from their grown-up work on computers
along with a fresh cup of free coffee
that someone else made for them.
A team of chefs prepared his lunch.
No one would puke on him.
He could sit alone in his office
or go to a meeting with other adults
who all wore real clothing
and had showered in the last two days.

I would make my own food all day,
feed the baby from my body
however many times she wanted to eat,
clean up everything, whatever it was—
poop, pee, breast milk, spit-up—
try to get my baby to nap,
and not see any other people.
If I had a few minutes of free time
I might do something really thrilling
like take the dog out or wash the dishes.
And no one would pay me.

At the follow-up breast ultrasound,
I drove to the back of the parking lot
and fed my baby one last time.
An empty breast would help them see
the mass was gone. I watched the rain
patter on the windshield while I fed her.
It rained every time I had an appointment.

I moved the car closer.
We checked in early,
then waited twenty minutes
while my breast quickly refilled.
We both got restless, so I pushed
the stroller back and forth
through a small hallway.
A man who was leaving
stopped to tell me,
"You're a good mom."
"Thanks," I replied, wondering
why he thought I needed to hear it.

I can never interpret ultrasound
scans, even of my own children.
Usually the technician can,
but she isn't allowed to say a word.
This time, neither of us had a clue.
It was white noise.

"I'm going to go get the doctor
so we can repeat the scan," she said.

I sat up and checked on the baby
who was for the moment
content in our cool, dark room.

The tech and radiologist returned
and she performed the scan again.
"Is it real?" the radiologist asked
as the tech searched through the haze.
"There. No, there! Yes.
That's real. Right on top
of that milk duct," he said.

The baby cried.
She had had enough.

"I'll talk to a colleague about this,"
said the radiologist, put off by the crying.
He shook my hand and left.

I picked up my crying baby and
changed her on the exam table.

I still have a mass.

We were halfway down
the covered walkway
when I noticed the rain shower
was now a total thunderstorm.
I turned back to the building.
The baby cried in her stroller.
The umbrella was in the car,
but it was impossible
to maneuver that stroller
while holding an umbrella.

I wished someone would
notice and offer to help.
I wished I had not urged
Caleb to go to work
instead of coming with us.
We waited and waited in the vestibule
until I couldn't wait anymore
and we ran to the car.
Baby cried as the rain hit her face.
"It's okay," I said. "Me too."

When anyone asks me,
"What's your favorite part?,"
I say it's when
she stares up at my face
after finishing her milk
and coos like she's talking
about her day at school,
the weird dream she had,
and how much she likes milk,
her panda, and the dog.

I WAS BREASTFEEDING ON THE COUCH
when I remembered it was the first day
of back-to-school in-service,
the one meeting I was on time for
during the entire school year.
In fact, I once arrived a full
twenty minutes early because
I was so excited to see my friends.

Now they were all there without me.

Later on, I would miss
a full inbox, being needed
by other people, being useful.

I couldn't see that
I was being useful.

I wrote down the day's
little accomplishments:
cut baby's fingernails,
made a smoothie,
fed baby ten times.

It still wasn't enough.

I apologized for the mess
when Caleb came home.

He never cared.
So why did I?

I FINISHED FEEDING THE BABY
and as I carried her to peek out
the front window I heard
splat, splat, splat.
I looked down.
Mustard-yellow islands
dotted the carpet.
This was my life.
I had a master's degree
but I couldn't get the diapers
to do the only thing
they were made to do.

IT'S BEEN TWELVE WEEKS
and I already want
another baby.

Why why why why why.

Dear Mrs. White,

Thank you for
your recent visit
to our facility.

Your breast imaging exam
showed an abnormality
that requires further follow up
by your health care provider.

Your first priority now
should be to complete
the testing of the abnormality.

You should make an appointment
with your health care provider
as soon as possible.

Sincerely,

Breast Imaging Department

"I tried to push it off
as long as I could,"
said the surgeon,
"but I don't feel comfortable
waiting any longer."

The nurse passed me
a *Breast Lumps* booklet
whose illustrated doctors and nurses
were locked in the 1980s.
She explained the biopsy procedure
and warned, "You can expect
some pretty spectacular bruising.
They could give you a valium
if you weren't breastfeeding."

Wouldn't that be nice.

I didn't fear cancer.
I was young with no
family history.
I feared instead
endless procedures,
needles, monitoring,
and medication.

Breast lump or no,
I was functional.
I had hoped each scan
would be the last.
But I had to keep going.

Please, God, give me courage.
Please let this be the end.

I KNEW THE BIOPSY WOULDN'T BE
as unpleasant as giving birth
or getting a lumbar puncture.
Still, I dreaded it all week.

In the waiting room—
under construction,
with areas sectioned off
by yellow caution tape—
an older couple bickered
about the number of fractures
in a cell phone X-ray image.

I could not sit. Too anxious.

They called my name.
Caleb and the baby
were allowed to come too.
The room was as bare as
a typical ultrasound room.
Three nurses bustled around
preparing the equipment.

One of the nurses explained
the order of events,
the radiologist arrived,
and the waiting ended
before I was ready.
I was cresting the top
of the roller coaster.

I put on an eye mask
and headphones.
I focused on breathing
and relaxing each muscle
in my face and neck,
but I couldn't do it.

The only pinch was the needle
for the lidocaine. I said, "Ouch."

The radiologist counted
to take the samples:
"One, two, three," *click,*
and a puff of air like a nail gun.

He apologized each time
he had to rest the tool on my chest
for the best angle, as if he had a choice,
as if I could say, "No. That placement
doesn't really work for me."

After three songs, it was over.

"Can I see what you took?" I asked.

"Sure," said the nurse. She held up
a plastic cup with the wormlike
shreds suspended in solution.

They cleaned me off, taped me up,
and stuck on a small ice pack.

I stopped shaking.

They promised to call in forty-eight hours.

THE NEXT MORNING WAS THE FIRST
mom and baby group.
We arrived fifteen minutes late.
I was always late before,
but now I had better excuses.

I had never been in a room
where every person was a mother.
Surely one of these forty mothers
could tell me where to buy baby shoes
and how to get my baby to nap.

I left baby sleeping in her stroller
and headed to the breakfast line.

The women at my table would become
my first mom friends. They would
teach me that it's polite to end a playdate
so naptime can begin. They would offer
to help when my baby had one of her
massive spit-ups at the emotional climax
of the speaker's talk. They would be there
when my baby developed an egg allergy.

I nursed uncovered but hid the incision.
I hadn't prepared an explanation.

I thought I was unique,
but later it turned out
we all bore marks.

AFTER WE GOT HOME FROM GROUP
blood seeped from the incision site
during the next feeding.
I soaked it up with a burp rag
and called the surgeon's office
where the nurse told me,
"It's probably just a hematoma,"
but I should come in the next day.

CLINICAL STAFF CALLED
later that day:

"Good news—it's a fibroadenoma.
A fibroadenoma is benign."

Hope flickered.

THE NEXT DAY AT THE SURGEON'S OFFICE
I fed baby, and blood-tinged milk
leaked from the incision site—
a milk fistula, of course.

The surgeon found me nursing
with a bloody, milky burp rag
stuck in the band of my bra.

She checked the incision site,
then left me lying on the table
to confer with a colleague.

At least I'm already
at the office this time.

When she returned, she re-taped
the incision site and said,
"I'm so sorry this happened."

"Thanks," I said. "How long
do you think it will last?"

"I'm not sure," she said.

Then she prescribed an empty breast.
I had to pump the right side during the night.

She then clarified: "We can ignore the fibroadenoma, but not the mastitis, which has persisted."

"What?" I said. "How could I still have it?"

"Likely it never went away," she said.

"But I took antibiotics for four weeks!" I said.

She shrugged and said, "I'll see you next week."

IN THE MIDDLE OF THE NIGHT
I carried the pumped milk
down to the fridge.
I opened the door,
and the lights faded on
with the celestial chorus
I always imagined,
but there was a problem.
The milk didn't look right.
I paused with one hand
on the handle of the fridge
and inspected the bottle.
The milk was pink,
strawberry-milk pink.

Oh, no.
Can my baby drink this?

I sent a side-by-side photo
of the pink and regular milk
to the pediatrician
and the surgeon.
Both said it was fine.

But after the milk was refrigerated
and the blood had settled on the bottom,
Caleb and I used the same syringes
from baby's early days to siphon
the white milk into fresh bottles.

WHEN I SAW THE SURGEON AGAIN,
she was pleased:
I had not leaked at all.
I had two ugly tape blisters
but no telltale infection redness.

I took the elevator up
to the parking garage.

There is nothing
wrong with me.

I wheeled baby to the car
and clicked her car seat in,

No more procedures.

loaded the stroller,

I'm free.

started the car,

I'm free.

and drove away.

I'm free!

AT FIFTEEN WEEKS
we go for a walk
just the two of us.
She notices trees
for the first time.
Her eyes follow
my eyes or my finger.
"There's a tree.
There's a big tree.
Do you see the tree?"
She grins at me like
it's the best day of her life.
Maybe it is.

ONE NIGHT LOOKING THROUGH PHOTOS,
I spotted one I hadn't seen before—
me holding the baby in my lap
when she visited the hospital.

"Did you know I took that?" Caleb asked.

"You thought I was going to die,"
I realized for the first time.

"I didn't know
what was going to happen," he said.

I printed this photo and kept it
in the drawer of my bedside table.

I will not die. I will live.

At an evening service
our pastor invited
anyone who wanted
prayer to walk forward.
I stood at the altar
with my palms up,
arms open. The hard things
passed in procession
through my mind
like a film reel
that I spread out
before God, asking:
"Do you see this cost?"
Then I felt in my body
before and above me
a heavy weight—
God the gentle
visiting me.
And I knew
that he did see.
An image came unbidden:
a side view of me
holding my baby
close to my chest.
"That's how I've got you," he said.
I stood with him,
palms up, arms open,
for a long time
and I didn't want to leave.

I CARTED BABY ACROSS TOWN
to watch spring come in
at Olbrich Gardens.

Willows glowed yellow-green.
Hyacinth and daffodils
dotted the grassy banks.
Her fingers reached
for bluebells.

Every week
a new flower,
every week
a little less baby.

TODAY MOTHERS AT CHURCH
smile at me in the hallway;
they can see I'm a coresident
in the land of sacrifice and wonder.

We rock, we soothe, inhale
peach baby smell, scribble
milestones, snap photos,
give up sleep,
give up more sleep,
give up even more sleep
until we fall asleep
on the ground during floor time.
We clean, we worry and fret,
give up drinking, cradle, shush,
play for hours with stacking cups,
shed our old selves and wait
for what we will next become.

One day's tribute isn't quite enough.

SHE IS ONE.
We splurge
on this party
and invite everyone
we've ever met.
This party is for us.
The theme is giraffes
because apparently
there must be a theme.
The same friend
who took care of her
when I was sick
builds a larger-than-life
balloon giraffe.
We order a triple-layer
banana-split sheet cake
with a baby giraffe design
that we will still be eating
out of the freezer
on her next birthday.
She presides
over the guests
like a queen
in her camping chair.
Everyone sings:
"Happy birthday,
dear Caroline,
Happy birthday
to you."

TEN DAYS LATER,
on my thirtieth birthday,
I remember where I was
on my last birthday,
and I am so grateful.

The next morning,
a tiny blue plus sign
smiles up at me.

Here we go again.

Afterword

I MADE THE FINAL edits to this book while being pregnant, giving birth, and breastfeeding for the third time. Having a newborn made the events described here feel fresh, but also distant. My biggest issue the first time around was lack of knowledge, especially in the area of breast care; I hadn't known how to treat engorgement or plugged ducts. The advice I received, whether from lactation consultants or the internet, was more harmful than helpful.

While preparing for my third child, I met an amazing lactation consultant named Polly. When I walked into her office, I noticed a poster that read "Breast Anatomy: Do *Not Massage* This Complex Gland!" She listened to my story, asked questions, and pulled up a video of a technique called lymphatic drainage. We made a plan for how I would manage the transition to lactation.

At first, I was somewhat skeptical about lymphatic drainage, but I was willing to try it. I could not believe how much of a difference it made; lymphatic drainage and icing for ten minutes after each feeding virtually eliminated engorgement when my milk came in. Stimulating lymphatic drainage takes only about thirty seconds but significantly reduces the amount of fluid and swelling in the breasts.[1]

Polly recommended the website run by Dr. Katrina Mitchell, a general surgeon, breast surgical oncologist, IBCLC lactation consultant and certified perinatal mental health provider (she's also a

---

1. Find a video demonstration called "Lymphatic Drainage for the Breast during Pregnancy and Lactation" at https://lacted.org/videos.

mom).[2] This website contains invaluable information about breast care, breastfeeding, mastitis, and mental health for mothers. My story might have been different if I had known about this resource.

While I'm not a healthcare provider, I share these tools in hope that they will make a difference for you or someone you know.

Cheering for you,

—*Sarah*

2 See physicianguidetobreastfeeding.org.

Acknowledgments

MANY PEOPLE HELPED BIRTH this book.

Thanks for initial excitement from first readers in my MOPS and neighborhood communities: Ashley, Rachel, Laura, Micah and Cassie, Lauren, and Tessa. Thank you to my friends for caring about this project: Agustina, Christina, Katie G., Katie J., Rachel, and Sarah S. Thank you for generously giving time and encouragement, Cameron Bellm, Christine Kindberg, and Deborah Sprinkle.

Thank you to my Redbud sisters, Prasanta Verma, Kendra Broekhuis, and Margaret Philbrick. For critical feedback, thank you to Julie Davis, Brittaini Maul, Laura Lundgren, and Geoffrey Hagberg. Thank you to Liz Grant, my book doula, for her incisive edits and for telling me *do not cancel*. Thank you to Matt Wimer at Wipf and Stock for patiently answering all of my questions.

Thank you to the nurses, doctors, and technicians at St. Mary's Hospital who cared for me with compassion and kindness. Thank you to Brent and María Benner.

Thank you to my teachers, Jeffry Davis, David Wright, Chad Davidson, and Gregory Fraser.

Thank you to everyone who made this book possible through their generous gifts of time and childcare: Caleb, Mom, Dad, Doug, Helen, Janaya, and Monica.

To my dad, thanks for always cheering me on. To my mom, I love our friendship.

Thank you to Caleb. Your steadfast presence and love are worth more than gold.

Thank you to God for never letting go.

Discussion Guide

1. Which parts of *Today I Left the House* resonated with you?

2. How did your baby's birth differ from your expectations?

3. Describe your adjustment to life with a newborn.

4. Did you face any unexpected curveballs in the first months of your baby's life?

5. If you experienced trauma, who or what were your best resources for processing it or for being healed?

6. What brought you hope in the midst of suffering?

7. What did you gain in your transition to motherhood (besides stretch marks)?

If You Liked This Book

- Consider leaving a review on Amazon or Goodreads.
- Sign up for Sarah's author newsletter at sarahmichellewhite.com/sign-up.
- Connect with Sarah on her website sarahmichellewhite.com or on Instagram @sarahmichellewhite.

Credits

Reiner, Rob, dir. *The Princess Bride.* DVD. Santa Monica, CA: MGM Home Entertainment, 2001. First released 1987.

www.ingramcontent.com/pod-product-compliance
Lightning Source LLC
Chambersburg PA
CBHW070826100426
42813CB00003B/502